Wha

Class never runs scare
knowledge that you car

Those who have class have wrestled with their own struggles and won a victory that marks them thereafter.
Class never makes excuses. It takes its lumps and learns from past mistakes.
Class is considerate of others. It knows that good manners are nothing more than a series of small sacrifices.
Class bespeaks an aristocracy that has nothing to do with ancestors or money. The most affluent blueblood can be totally without class while the descendant of a Welsh miner may ooze class from every pore.
Class never tries to build itself up by tearing others down. Class is already up and need not strive to look better by making others look worse.
Class can "walk with kings and keep its virtue and talk with crowds and keep the common touch." Everyone is comfortable with the person who has class because he is comfortable with himself.
If you have class you don't need much of anything else. If you don't have it, no matter what else you have, it doesn't make much difference.

Jacob Helm – Class of 2021

From: Coach P.

Inspiration for the Graduate is without a doubt the most meaningful and economical gift I've ever given to my graduating high-school seniors/student athletes. Rather than a generic card and gift card to a fast-food joint or coffee shop, why not give the graduate something that they can refer back to for years to come? The ability to write a hand-written note on the inside allows for personalization, and then the graduate is ready to start turning pages and reading inspirational quotes from the likes of Bobby Knight, Coach K, John Wooden and more. As a long-time teacher and coach, I highly recommend considering giving this book as a gift to graduating seniors.

—Scott Steinbrook,
Kearney (NE) High School
Head Boys Basketball Coach,
Head Boys Soccer Coach

Inspiration for the Graduate is fantastic! Reading this book has made me a better teacher and coach. The messages contained will not only help to guide the graduate to success, but will also inspire anyone who reads to reach new levels of success. I highly recommend this book to anyone who is driven to achieve.

—Kyle Elmendorf,
High School Football
and Basketball Coach

Hey Coach! The skills and life lessons you have taught me throughout my sports career have not only made me a better player but also a better person. I turn to this book whenever I need inspiration and wisdom. I can't thank you enough for what you've done for me.

—Landon Willyerd,
Park High School Team Member,
Graduating Class of 2012

INSPIRATION for the GRADUATE

Thoughts & Quotes from the World of Athletics to Enhance the Next Stage of Your Life

Coach Scott Rosberg

Coach with Character
Livingston, Montana

ISBN 978-0-9961320-0-8 (print)

ISBN 978-0-9961320-1-5 (e-book)

1. Sports & Recreation / General

2. Self-Help / Motivational & Inspirational

More information and additional copies from

Scott Rosberg
Coach with Character

110 Altair Drive
Livingston, Montana 59047

Available through Amazon.com
and at ScottRosberg.com

Cover and layout by Denis Ouellette

Printed in the United States of America

Contents

Preface 8

For the Graduate 12

Acknowledgments 18

WORK ETHIC 21

DISCIPLINE 27

POISE .33

ENTHUSIASM 39

CONFIDENCE 45

PERSEVERANCE 51

WINNING & LOSING 57

ADAPTABILITY 65

COURAGE 71

LEADERSHIP 79

Bibliography 85

About the Author 87

Preface

This book is written for the graduate. However, as you peruse it, you will notice a large emphasis on the athletic world. While I originally planned to write it for the athletes who I have coached, I realized that there are many more graduates out there than just "my athletes" who can enjoy and learn from the ideas and quotes in here. So while the majority of the quotes and ideas can be viewed from an athletic perspective, the thought behind them or the message that they are delivering can certainly be far greater than just something dealing with sports.

If you are one of my players, let me say, "Thank you" for all you have done for me through our time together. As a teacher and coach, I am charged with trying to help young people learn all kinds of things to help them go out and make their way in the world. However, I learned early in my career that I was learning as much, if not more, from "my kids" as they were learning from me. I have also received great joy from my relationship with each of you. Coaching has been one of the great joys of my life, and it is because of getting to work and play with people like you that it has been so much fun. I hope you enjoy reading the quotes and ideas in this book as much as I have enjoyed making it for you. Please stay in touch with me through the years. I would love to know where life takes you. One of the tougher things about teaching and coaching is that, unlike people who make products, we don't see the finished product of our effort. We send you off for more developing and growth. So it is always nice to hear from former players and students to see where life has taken them.

If you are a former student or player of mine from years gone by, and you somehow have gotten a copy of this book, I hope you are well. As I just said in the last paragraph to my current crop of graduating players, I don't always know how life turned out for you or where life has taken you. Feel free to drop me a line some time and let me know. I'd love to hear from you. You helped shape me in our time together, and I would like to thank you for the part you played in that. If you have a child of your own who is graduating and you are giving him or her this book, thanks for thinking that it might be something that he or she might benefit from. I hope it does just that.

If you are a total stranger to me and someone is giving you this book for your graduation, congratulations on this great moment! While I don't know you, I hope that you can take something from this book as you move on in your life. Chances are you were or are an athlete, and that is why someone has given you this book. I hope athletics or some other extra-curricular activity has helped you through the years to become the person that you are right now. Athletics offers many life lessons, as I'm sure you have already learned. But it is only through intentional and purposeful teaching of those lessons that we can know for sure if those lessons are being taught. I hope you enjoy the lessons that the ideas and quotes in here are designed to teach and inspire. I also encourage you, as I encouraged my players above, to stay in touch with your coaches and whoever gave you this book. It is one of the great rewards of teaching and coaching to see our kids grow up and make their way in the world, and we love hearing about all that they do. Good luck to you as you take the next step of your life.

To all of you, keep playing the games that have been a part of your life for as long as you can, keep trying new games as you continue on through life, and keep learning all that the games you play and the people with whom you play them have to teach you!

—Scott Rosberg

For the Graduate

This book has been many years in the making. By that I don't mean that it is something I have been writing for many years. Rather I mean that I couldn't have written this book without being a teacher and coach for the many years that I have done so. It is the 25+ years of experience in education that has brought me to this point where I feel I must write this for those students who are graduating from high school and moving on to college, careers, families, and all that life has to offer them. I have contemplated doing this for quite a few years, but the time when I seem to think about it the most is the week or two before graduation at the school at which I work, and by then it is too late.

Well, to be honest, I'm not in a much better situation right now. We are THREE WEEKS from graduation at Park High School in Livingston, Montana where I am the Activities/Athletic Director and Boys' Head

Basketball Coach. However, I have some time to put this together and get it published, and I figured, "Now is the time!"

So why a book for graduates? Because for the 28 years that I have been involved in the world of education, I have struggled to find something meaningful to give to "my kids" that I have taught and coached or with whom I have had some type of adult/student relationship. Each year I buy a card and some type of gift card that I hope the young man or woman can use as he or she steps out into the next phase of life.

In some years, I have upwards of ten students/athletes to whom I give something, which means I have ten cards that I have to try to find that say the things I believe are important for a young person moving on in the world. However, I must also try to do this without giving the same card to all of them since most of them know each other, and I would feel they might think I didn't really consider my words to them, if the words were the same for all of them.

The other reason is strictly one of economics. As a teacher/coach, I do not knock down the biggest bucks in the earning department, and buying anywhere from five to fifteen $25.00 gift cards can get down-right expensive. Also, it again becomes a problem of finding "the right one" for each person. Also, the sentimentalist in me believes that, while buying something for $25.00 at Target or Cabela's might help these kids out now, what I really hope to do is help them for much longer than a laundry basket and towels for college or some new fishing lures will last them. My hope is that they will find some inspiration from some of the quotes and ideas in here that can help them deal with some of the things that life is going to throw their way.

I also hope that maybe five, ten, twenty years down the road, as they are moving into a new house and packing up the bookcase or the closet into boxes, they will come across this book and remember the time that we/they spent together as part of a family, team, school, or whatever that relationship was founded on.

For those of you who are receiving this who I did not coach, or who I don't know all that well, or who I don't even know at all, I hope that you find something in here, too, that helps you with whatever life throws at you. For my entire life after I started walking, I have been involved with sports. From playing in parks, streets, and driveways with friends, to playing on organized teams through high school and college, and then coaching teams for over twenty-five years, athletics has always been part of my life.

I have found great inspiration, comfort, excitement, passion, and joy through athletics. I have also found many of the lessons of life that have helped me the most came to me through my various athletic experiences. One of my main goals as a coach has been to help young people learn many of those types of lessons through sports, just like I have.

So throughout all my years of coaching, I have tried to give players various lessons, motivational quotes, team themes, and teachable moments that might help them deal with our team/sport situations, but more importantly, help them deal with life. This book is a direct result of all of those kinds of lessons and moments that I have tried to help my students and athletes learn and enjoy. I hope that you, too, will find something in here that you can learn and enjoy.

Congratulations on your graduation! It is one of the many landmark moments that you will have in your life. However, the key to many landmark moments is not what you have just done, but what you are going to do now. Not to sound trite, but while graduation is the end of something, it truly is the beginning of something else. What that something else is for you is unknown.

Oh sure, you may have your next step planned out, like going to college or starting to work, but you really never know if that plan is going to go the way you have it planned out. In my English classes, I used to teach a poem by a Scottish poet named Robert Burns called, "To a Mouse," about a farmer who has plowed up a mouse's house in autumn. His poem is a bit of an apology to the mouse, for he realizes the mouse must now find a new home for his family, and the cold and snow of winter is right around the corner. But the line that the poem hinges on (in its more modern English version) is, "the best laid plans of mice and men, sometimes go awry."

Maybe you have read this poem in one of your English classes. Or maybe you read the John Steinbeck novel *Of Mice and Men*, for which Steinbeck took the title from the Burns poem. Whether you have or have not read either of these, the message is still there for all of us—no matter how much you plan things out, understand that life has a way of throwing curves at you, and you can really never know exactly how things will go. Be flexible and adaptable. As the principal, Gary Kane, at the school I work at now often says, (quoting the gunnery sergeant in the Clint Eastwood movie *Heartbreak Ridge*), "We must improvise, adapt, and overcome." Get ready to do a lot of improvising, adapting, and overcoming for the next, well, let's just say for the rest of your life. And it starts with the next step of your life.

Enjoy this monumental moment in your life. But don't stop there. Enjoy all the moments of your life, and make each of them monumental in their own way. There's a whole world and a big future out there waiting for you. What you do with it is all up to you. Live it to the fullest!

Acknowledgments

I would like to give special thanks to Bruce Brown, the director of Proactive Coaching, for his help with the ideas in this book. The majority of the ideas and quotes came from his book, *1001 Motivational Messages and Quotes for Athletes and Coaches: Teaching Character Through Sport* (Coaches Choice, 2001), and I highly recommend you pick up a copy of this outstanding book for more great ideas and quotes. Coach Brown has been a huge mentor to me, as well as thousands of other coaches, kids, and parents across the country. I recommend you check out any of the books, booklets, CDs, or DVDs that he has produced on the topic of character-based athletics and coaching. He can be reached at ProactiveCoaching.info. Also, check out Proactive Coaching's Facebook page and join the 150,000+ coaches, athletes, and parents who are receiving coaching/athletic nuggets daily.

This past year my basketball team worked our way through the Pyramid of Success that legendary basketball coach John Wooden developed. We took a building block or two each week and discussed it and stressed that concept for each game for that week, working our way up the Pyramid throughout the year. This was a great experience for our boys, and they all have said how much they loved going through the lessons of the Pyramid. The book I used for this was Coach Wooden's *Pyramid of Success* (Wooden & Carty, Regal Books, 2005). There are many books and versions of the Pyramid of Success out there, but this one did a nice job of explaining Coach Wooden's ideas behind the blocks of the Pyramid. Thanks to Coach Wooden for all he contributed to our world.

Mike Krzyzewski's book *Leading with the Heart* has also been used in the creation of this book. Coach K has been a source of a lot of learning for me, from his basketball X's and O's to his works on leadership like in *Leading with the Heart*. Thanks to Coach K for inspiration throughout all of my years as a basketball coach and for a couple of the quotes in here from his book.

WORK ETHIC

As you embark on the next phase of your life, one of the most important character traits you can have is a strong work ethic. Whether you are going to continue your education, you are going into the military, or you are joining the work force, the ability to work hard is going to be crucial to your success. (Just look at your choices—some kind of school, which is at least two years of continuing your studies; military, working to protect our country; or the work force, where "work" is in the name of what you are doing!) As an athlete, you were expected to give your best effort every day to help your team have its best chance at success. But along with the physical part of having a strong work ethic came focus, initiative, and attention to detail. When you develop strong work habits, you can accomplish so much more in life, both individually and as a team. While working hard does not come naturally, when you make working hard a normal part of your everyday existence, you set yourself up for success in all you do.

"The harder you work, the harder it is to surrender."

—Vince Lombardi
Professional Football Coach

"Opportunity is missed by most people because it is dressed in overalls and looks like work."

—Thomas Edison,
Inventor

"I'm a great believer in luck, and I find the harder I work, the more I have of it."

—Thomas Jefferson,
United States President

"Industriousness is the most conscientious, assiduous, and inspired type of work. A willingness to, an appetite for, hard work must be present for success. Without it, you have nothing to build on."

—John Wooden,
College Basketball Coach

"Working hard becomes a habit, a serious kind of fun. You get self-satisfaction from pushing yourself to the limit, knowing that all the effort is going to pay off."

—Mary Lou Retton,
US Olympic Gymnast

"One of life's most painful moments comes when we must admit that we didn't do our homework, that we are not prepared."

—Merlin Olsen,
NFL Lineman

"Do not confuse activity with achievement."

—John Wooden,
College Basketball Coach

"Spectacular achievements are always preceded by unspectacular preparation."

—Roger Staubach,
NFL Quarterback

DISCIPLINE

Discipline is having a focused attention and effort. It is doing what needs to be done, doing it the proper way to accomplish the task at hand, and doing it that way every time one is working to accomplish that task. Sometimes, though, there is no task—there is just living your life. When speaking of discipline in this situation, one has to have the discipline to live one's life as he should in order to be all that he can be.

Too often, discipline is looked at as a dirty word thought of in terms of punishment. Discipline is actually a positive term & personal characteristic. Discipline is a choice. One who has discipline has chosen to do all that is necessary to succeed, whatever that entails. The disciplined person doesn't just stay up late studying for an exam the next day (although that may be required to help achieve success on the exam). The disciplined student pays attention in class, reads the required reading (and often more than just what is required), takes notes, studies the notes, and works toward an understanding of the material long before the night before the exam. The disciplined worker shows up at the job site on time, knows what needs to be done and does it without being told or reminded, and sees the job through until its completion. Discipline carries people and it carries teams to heights unattainable without it.

"Discipline is: knowing what to do,
knowing when to do it,
doing it to the best of your abilities,
and doing it that way
every single time."

—Bobby Knight,
College Basketball Coach

"It doesn't matter what you're trying
to accomplish. It's all a matter
of discipline."

—Wilma Rudolph,
US Olympic Sprinter

**"I believe in discipline.
You can forgive incompetence.
You can forgive lack of ability.
But one thing you cannot ever forgive
is lack of discipline."**

*—Forrest Gregg,
NFL Lineman*

**"The sterner the discipline,
the greater the devotion."**

*—Pete Carill,
College Basketball Coach*

**"Without self-discipline,
success is impossible... period."**

*—Lou Holtz,
College Football Coach*

"Discipline helps you finish a job, and finishing is what separates excellent work from average work. Discipline yourself, so no one else has to."

—Pat Summitt,
Women's College Basketball Coach

"If my players work hard every day, then they won't have to worry about game plans, or where they play, or whom they play, or about rankings, and so on. They have their daily behavior—their discipline—to fall back on."

—Pete Carill,
College Basketball Coach

POISE

Most of us think of poise as controlling one's emotions while maintaining a calm demeanor and a self-assured dignity. The person with poise can maintain a sense of composure when things are not going well or not going as planned. While this ability is extremely helpful for individuals to be able to achieve their goals, it is crucial for success in any team or group setting. When teammates see others reacting to stressful situations with poise, it gives the rest of the team the confidence it needs to deal with the situation. Conversely, when teammates see one another displaying anger, temper, or frustration, it ratchets up everyone's anxiety. Teammates start to question their ability to succeed, and they start focusing energy on the person or people who are "losing it." This hurts the ability of the team to rise above the problem at hand and deal with it in such a way to create success. Be a person who shows poise in the midst of chaos. Be the face your team needs to see. Coach Wooden calls poise "just being you." He says, that people who have poise are "not acting, faking, or pretending. When we are being who we really are, we'll have a greater likelihood of functioning nearer our own level of competency.

"Poise and confidence will come from conditioning, skill, and team spirit. To have poise and be truly confident, you must be in condition and know you are fundamentally sound, and possess the proper team attitude."

—John Wooden,
College Basketball Coach

"The only way to maximize potential for performance is to be calm in the mind."

—Brian Sipe,
NFL Quarterback

"The key to winning is poise under stress."

—Paul Brown, Professional Football Coach

"When I play, I'm boiling inside. I just try not to show it because it's a lack of composure, and if you give in to your emotions after one loss, you're liable to have three or four in a row."

—Chris Evert, Professional Tennis Player

"Anger is just one letter short of danger."

—Unknown

"When you lose control of your emotions, when your self-discipline breaks down, your judgment and common sense suffer. How can you perform at your best when you are using poor judgment?"

—John Wooden,
College Basketball Coach

"Losing your head in a crisis is a good way to become the crisis."

C.J. Redwine,
Author of Defiance

"People ask me what makes a great skier. It takes the gift; but besides the gift, it takes that availability of the mind, which permits total control of all the elements that lead to victory—total composure."

—Jean-Claude Killy,
Professional Skier

ENTHUSIASM

Enthusiasm is a critical component of anyone involved in any worthwhile endeavor. It is critical to success for someone to possess enthusiasm for whatever they are involved in. From school to sports to work, those with enthusiasm bring more to the experience, both for themselves and for others. Enthusiasm is catching. When people see and hear others displaying enthusiasm, it spreads to all involved.

Unfortunately, that also can happen with people who do not have enthusiasm. These people can drain the enthusiasm right out of a team, a group of friends, a company, or anywhere else people are together. It is better to not let such people have much of a voice in group settings. Rather, give voice to all those who have the passion for the task at hand. When people choose to be enthusiastic, they up their own output, and they help spread excitement to others in the organization.

Put your heart and soul into all you do and let it show to the world around you. You, and the people who you touch in your life, will be glad you did.

"Success is not the result
of spontaneous combustion.
You must set yourself on fire."

—Reggie Leach,
Hockey Player

"Enthusiasm is the fire in our furnace.
It is the spark that keeps us going
in high gear. It makes going great.

Enthusiasm brings on Excitement;
Excitement then produces Energy;
Energy generates Extra Effort;
Extra Effort develops Excellence."

—Frosty Westering,
College Football Coach

"The successful man has enthusiasm. Good work is never done in cold blood; heat is needed to forge anything. Every great achievement is the story of a flaming heart."

Harry Truman,
United States President

"If you aren't fired with enthusiasm, you'll be fired with enthusiasm."

—Vince Lombardi,
Professional Football Coach

"I probably have a different mental approach to swimming than most people. I actually enjoy the training."

—Dawn Fraser,
Olympic Swimmer

**"Merit begets confidence;
confidence begets enthusiasm;
enthusiasm conquers the world."**

*—Walter Cottingham,
Former CEO Sherwin-Williams*

**"I am the greatest builder in the world.
I am the foundation of every triumph.
No matter what your position is,
I can better it. My name is enthusiasm."**

—Anonymous

**"It is more probable that your attitude,
rather than your aptitude,
will determine your altitude in life."**

—Unknown

CONFIDENCE

Confidence comes from a few different sources. Some people just seem to have confidence from the time they are born. However, confidence itself is not a quality that one is born with. It takes preparation and success to have confidence become a part of one's character. The truly confident person is prepared. He realizes that any future success is only going to occur by preparing properly for the chance to create the outcome he seeks. He realizes that, while hope and prayer have their merits, the only sure-fire way to create the best chance at success is to prepare for it.

The student who doesn't pay attention in class, take notes, study regularly, get enough rest, and then crams for a test the night before (see Discipline), is not prepared properly, and hence, will not go into the exam with the same level of confidence as the one who has taken care of all those things. The athlete who focuses, practices hard, pays attention to the scouting report, works hard in the weight room, eats properly, and gets the right amount of rest will walk into the arena knowing that she is ready to perform at her best. She may win, or she may lose, but the outcome will not be affected for her by a lack of preparation.

This kind of confidence is not always easily understood by younger people and athletes. Too often, they see other people pounding their chests and talking loudly to try and show how confident they are. Usually, these people are actually not very confident at all, so they try to cover up their insecurities about their lack of preparation for the event by talking big. The truly confident person carries himself with a quiet, peaceful inner confidence that says, "I have prepared well for this, so I know that I can perform well."

The other quality that breeds confidence is success. Those who have experienced success before generally feel confident that they can achieve it again. Interestingly, these people's confidence may carry over into other areas of their lives where they have not had success before, but because they understand the importance of preparation for success in one realm, they can see its value in all of the realms of their lives. But again, it all comes back to preparation. The prepared person is a confident person.

"Confidence comes from being prepared."

—John Wooden, College Basketball Coach

"Basketball is just something else to do, another facet of life. I'm going to be a success at whatever I choose because of my preparation. By the time the game starts, the outcome has been decided. I never think about having a bad game because I have been prepared."

—David Robinson, NBA Center

"Valor and confidence grow by being daring; fear and failure by holding back."

—Unknown

"The biggest mistake an athlete can make is to be afraid to make one."

—L. Ron Hubbard,
Author

"There is a difference between conceit and confidence. A quarterback has to have confidence. Conceit is bragging about yourself. Confidence means you believe you can get the job done. I have always believed that I could get the job done."

—Johnny Unitas,
NFL Quarterback

"It is never an upset if the so-called underdog has all along considered itself the better team."

—Woody Hayes,
College Football Coach

PERSEVERANCE

Life is going to throw curves at you. We all experience ups and downs, good and bad, success and failure. But to not risk failure is setting oneself up for failure. Risking failure is a key to working through things and eventually succeeding. The young athlete who only works on his strengths because "he can't" do the moves that are his weaknesses, is setting himself up for problems down the road. When the time comes for him that he has to have another move to go to, he will fail, because he has failed to fight through the difficulty and fear of failing at that move. Perseverance is about staying the course when things get tough. It is having the mental toughness to fight through difficult circumstances. It is having the ability to recover quickly enough from some mistake to get oneself back on the road to success. As you make your way through college, the military, or the work world, understand that there will be problems along the way. Don't let the problems stop you from moving to where you want to go. Get back up quickly, dust yourself off, and attack your situation with the same determination that you had before your setback. Not only will you be showing perseverance, but you will also be another step closer to the goal you are seeking.

"Our greatest weakness lies in giving up. The most certain way to success is always to try just one more time."

—Thomas Edison, Inventor

"The man who wins may have been counted out several times, but didn't hear the referee."

—H.E. Jackson

"Face your deficiencies and acknowledge them. But do not let them master you."

—Helen Keller, Author, Activist, Lecturer

"Failure is an opportunity to begin again, more intelligently."

—Henry Ford, Inventor & Auto Maker

"Giving up reinforces our sense of incompetence; going on gives you a commitment to success."

—George Weinberg, Psychologist

"Things that hurt, instruct."

—Ben Franklin, Founding Father

"Everybody is looking for instant success, but it doesn't work that way. You build a successful life one day at a time."

—Lou Holtz, College Football Coach

"The difference between the possible and the impossible lies in one's determination."

—Tommy Lasorda, Baseball Manager

"Failure is only postponed success, as long as courage 'coaches' ambition. The habit of persistence is the habit of victory."

—Herbert Kaufman, Author

"Character cannot be developed in ease and quiet. Only through experiences of trial and suffering can the soul be strengthened, vision cleared, ambition inspired, and success achieved."

—Helen Keller, Author, Activist, Lecturer

CHARGERS
10
CHARGERS
80
60
69

WINNING & LOSING

Too often young people and people involved in athletics focus way too much on the scoreboard as a determiner of success. While the scoreboard is there for a reason and winning the game is a goal of competition, there is so much more to success than just winning a game. With all the teams I have coached through the years, I tried to instill in them a focus on many more things that determine if we were successful: how hard we played, how smart we played, how well we played together, whether we achieved our potential. Too often people compare themselves to others. I tried to instill in my players the idea that they should compete against a vision of their best selves and that we should compete against a vision of what we could be as the best team we were capable of becoming.

I also have always tried to instill in players that how we deal with winning and losing is just as important with the winning and losing itself. When we win, that's great, but we must not let it affect our humility, our attitude toward ourselves and others, or our ability to turn around and prepare for the next challenge. Sometimes, dealing with victory can be much more difficult than dealing with loss. How we deal with losing will determine a whole lot about who we are and who we have the potential to become. We must not take a loss as the end of the world. It is a chance for us to see where we need improvement, and then to get back to work on making the necessary changes for that improvement. Do not get too high when you win or too low when you lose. Remember that every day that you wake up and get out of bed, you will be moving one way or the other—toward success or failure. The choice of which direction you go is one that you make every day.

**"Success is peace of mind
that is the direct result
of self-satisfaction in knowing
you did your best to become the best
that you are capable of becoming."**

*—John Wooden,
College Basketball Coach*

"We play with enthusiasm and recklessness. We aren't afraid to lose. If we win, great. But win or lose, it is the competition that gives us pleasure."

—Joe Paterno,
College Football Coach

"The 'final score' is not the final score. My final score is how prepared you were to execute near your own particular level of competence, both individual and as a team."

—John Wooden,
College Basketball Coach

"Handle success like you handle failure. You can't always control what happens, but you can control how you handle it."

—Pat Summitt,
Women's College Basketball Coach

"I pray not for victory, but to do my best."

—Amos Alonzo Stagg,
College Football Coach

"Success isn't something that just happens—success is learned, success is practiced, and then it is shared."

—Sparky Anderson,
Professional Baseball Manager

"Don't be afraid to fail. Experience is just mistakes you don't make anymore."

—Joe Garagiola,
Professional Baseball Player

"How a man plays the game shows something of his character; how he loses shows all of it."

—Frosty Westering, College Football Coach

"If you keep doing things the way you have always done them, you will keep getting whatever you have gotten."

—Unknown

"Losing is only temporary and not all encompassing. You must simply study it, learn from it, and try hard not to lose the same way again. Then you must have the self-control to forget about it."

—John Wooden, College Basketball Coach

"Many times, the best way to learn is through mistakes. A fear of making mistakes can bring individuals to a standstill, to a dead center. Fear is the wicked want that transforms human beings into vegetables."

—George Brown,
Newspaper Publisher

"The wonderful thing about the game of life is that winning and losing are only temporary— unless you quit."

—Unknown

ADAPTABILITY

The ability to adapt to the various situations one finds oneself in is important in all aspects of life. In athletics, it is critical to team and individual success because athletic endeavors are fraught with adversity, and the adversity comes in many forms. People need to understand the importance of being flexible with regards to the variety of things that get thrown at them. On any given day, in any given situation, a person may have to deal with a myriad of problems and dilemmas that could affect his or her focus on the task at hand. The ability to adapt to problems is crucial to getting through those problems and growing from them.

Another important part of adaptability is the idea that people need to adapt to each other and to the teams or groups they are part of. When people are selfless and they give up a part of themselves for the good of others, they are showing their adaptability to something bigger than themselves. When people sacrifice their own personal agendas and egos for the establishment of a stronger, joint team ego, they are saying that the team's goals are more important than their own individual goals. However, that is not to say that they must give up every part of themselves and their egos. There is a reason they are on the team, and they must contribute their strengths to the team for the team to succeed. Everyone brings something to the table, and it is important for everyone to realize that each member of the team offers some things to the team, while at the same time giving some things up for the team. This goes for the leaders as well. Leaders need to understand that they, too, must adapt. Everyone, including the leader, needs to have the flexibility to adapt for the good of all. When all members of a team, group, or family understand the importance of maximizing their strengths while giving of themselves selflessly, anything is possible.

"Everyone in this world is dealt a different hand—some better, some worse than others—but what's more important is how you play that hand. This is what builds character. And with great character comes great reward."

—Christine Ha,
Blind Chef & Author

"The art of life is a constant readjustment to our surroundings."

—K. Okakaura, Japanese Author

"Learn to adjust yourself to the conditions you have to endure, but make a point of trying to alter or correct the conditions so that they are most favorable to you."

—William Frederick Book, Psychology Professor

"Enjoying success requires the ability to adapt. Only by being open to change will you have a true opportunity to get the most from your talent."

—Nolan Ryan, Professional Baseball Player

"You have to adapt what you do based on who you are."

—Mike Krzyzewski, College Basketball Coach

"A leader needs to be a part of a mutual adaptation that forms a combination of the best of everyone."

—Mike Krzyzewski, College Basketball Coach

"The more you adapt, the more interesting you are."

—Martha Stewart

COURAGE

Courage is oftentimes a misunderstood word, and it is especially misunderstood by young people. So often, people believe that courage is something that is dramatic or newsworthy, like running into a burning building to save a baby. While that certainly is a courageous act, courage occurs in many other instances in life that are not anywhere near so dramatic, and yet can be almost as important for the people involved. True courage is often seen in the everyday elements of life, the decisions that people make on a regular basis. These decisions can be those that are made alone or in groups and teams.

As we explore the concepts of courage, we start to see that courage is all around us, and there are many moments that provide opportunities for us to display courage. As athletes start to recognize courage in their own lives and the lives of their teammates, they start to see it in other walks of life. They "come to understand that most people have far more courage than they give themselves credit for in most situations. Once discovered in themselves, acts of courage are easier to repeat. Once seen in others, teammates, family, and friends, courageous choices are more appreciated and modeled." (Bruce Brown, 1001 Motivational Messages and Quotes for Athletes and Coaches: Teaching Character Through Sport, Coaches Choice, 2001).

Choose to live courageously every day by making the right decisions that affect everyone in the best way possible. As you embark on the next journey of your life, courage will be a companion that will suit you well. You will need to have the courage to not just step out into the unknown, but to jump into it with both feet, even though you are unsure of where you will land.

"To reach out for another
is to risk involvement.

To expose one's feelings
is to risk exposing your true self.

To place your ideas, your dreams,
before a crowd is to risk their loss.

To love is to risk
not being loved in return.

To live is to risk dying.
To hope is to risk despair.
To try is to risk failure.

But risks must be taken, because the
greatest hazard in life is to risk nothing.

The people who risk nothing, do
nothing, have nothing, and are nothing.

They may avoid suffering and sorrow, but
they cannot learn, feel,
change, grow, love, live.

Chained by their attitudes,
they are slaves, they have forfeited
their freedom.

Only a person who risks is free."

—Unknown

"Man cannot discover new oceans unless he has the courage to lose sight of the shore."

—Andre Gide,
Author & Nobel Prize Winner

"Courage is reckoned the greatest of all virtues; because, unless a man has that virtue, he has no security for preserving any other."

—Samuel Johnson,
English Author

"One man with courage makes a majority."

—Andrew Jackson,
United States President

"To see what is right and not to do it, is lack of courage."

—Confucius,
Chinese Philosopher

**"Courage doesn't always roar.
Sometimes courage is the little voice
at the end of the day that says
I'll try again tomorrow."**

*—Mary Anne Radmacher,
Author*

**"Courage is resistance to fear,
mastery of fear—
not absence of fear."**

—Anonymous

**"Being courageous requires
no exceptional qualifications,
no magic formula, no special
combination of time, place and
circumstance. It is an opportunity
that sooner or later
is presented to us all."**

*—John F. Kennedy,
United States President*

"Courage is the first of human qualities because it is the quality which guarantees all the others."

—Sir Winston Churchill,
British Prime Minister

"One isn't necessarily born with courage, but one is born with potential. Without courage, we cannot practice any other virtue with consistency. We can't be kind, true, merciful, generous, or honest."

—Maya Angelou,
American Poet & Author

"Three daily reminders:
Have the courage to say 'No.'
Have the courage to face the truth.
Have the courage to do the right thing because it is right."

—W. Clement Stone,
Author

LEADERSHIP

A leader needs to learn to lead in a variety of ways. Leadership is not about telling other people what to do. The best leaders realize they are there to serve those they lead. Leadership is about helping others to realize the potential they have, and then helping them to rise up to that potential and achieve what they are capable of. But leadership does not have to come from one person in an organization. In fact, the best organizations have multiple leaders at multiple levels. In athletics, while the head coach is the ultimate leader, there are assistant coaches who lead as well.

Then there are players who have natural leadership tendencies that allow them to lead their teammates. Finally, sometimes, certain players are bestowed the title of captain, giving them a responsibility to lead the members of the team. However, any and all members of a team can be leaders, no matter the organization and no matter who the individuals are in that organization. It is critical for the ultimate leaders of the organization to recognize the importance of letting the natural leadership of various individuals within the organization come to the forefront. It is also important for the leader to sometimes recognize that he or she has to cultivate that leadership to come forward.

"The wise leader is of service:
receptive, yielding, following.
The group's members' vibration
dominates and leads, while the leader
follows. But soon, it is the members'
consciousness which is transformed.
It is the job of the leader to be aware
of the group's members' process;
it is the need of the group member
to be received and paid attention to.
Both get what they need, if the leader
has the wisdom to serve and follow."

—John Heider,
Author of The Tao of Leadership

"Leadership must be demonstrated, not announced."

—Fran Tarkenton,
NFL Quarterback

"Try to set standards that will make other people wish they were on your team."

—Ken Horne,
Comedian & Businessman

"A good leader is a person who takes a little more than his share of the blame and a little less than his share of the credit."

—John C. Maxwell,
Author & Leadership Guru

"Nothing so conclusively proves a man's ability to lead others as what he does from day to day to lead himself."

—Thomas J. Watson,
Former CEO of IBM

"Great teams have multiple leaders, multiple voices. A major part of building a team is discovering who those voices will be and cultivating them, making sure that their leadership is established within your group."

—Mike Krzyzewski,
College Basketball Coach

"Leaders are chosen to serve; there is always trouble when a leader forgets this."

—Unknown

**"If he works for you,
you work for him."**

—Japanese Proverb

**"Never doubt that a small group
of thoughtful, committed citizens
can change the world.
Indeed, it is the only thing
that ever has."**

*—Margaret Mead,
Cultural Anthropologist*

Bibliography

Brown, Bruce Eamon. *1001 Motivational Messages and Quotes for Athletes and Coaches: Teaching Character Through Sport.* Coaches Choice, 2001.

Brown, Bruce Eamon. *Another 1001 Motivational Messages and Quotes: The Seven Essentials of Great Teams.* Coaches Choice, 2003.

Krzyzewski, Mike. *Leading with the Heart.* Warner Business Books, 2001.

Wooden, John & Jay Carty. *Coach Wooden's Pyramid of Success.* Regal Books, 2005

About the Author

Scott Rosberg is currently the boys' head basketball coach for Park High School in Livingston, Montana. He has been coaching at the high-school level for over 25 years, and he has been an athletic director for 11 years. He has coached both boys and girls of all ages in basketball, football, and soccer, in Illinois, Montana, and Washington state. In addition to *Inspiration for the Graduate*, he has published seven coaching booklets:

- *A Head Coach's Guide to Working with Assistants*
- *The Assistant Coach's Guide to Coaching*
- *Playing Time: A Guide for Coaches, Athletes & Parents*
- *Establishing Your Coaching Philosophy*

- *Team & Program Policies: Elements to Consider*
- *The Sportsmanship Dilemma*
- *The Responsibilities of Coaching*

Scott does workshops and presentations at schools and coaching clinics on these topics and more. He is also a member of the **Proactive Coaching** team of speakers. Proactive Coaching works with coaches, athletes, leaders and teams by providing presentations and published materials designed to make a positive difference and be immediately applicable. Proactive Coaching assists individuals, teams and organizations to intentionally create, change, or restore a culture of excellence and reach their full potential in both competence and character. Proactive Coaching can be found on the web at ProactiveCoaching.info.

Scott can be reached through his website:

ScottRosberg.com

or by email at
scott@ProactiveCoaching.info

Made in the USA
Middletown, DE
21 April 2021